MY FIRST BOOK

CHINA

ALL ABOUT CHINA FOR KIDS

GLOBED
CHILDREN BOOKS

Interior and cover Design: Daniel Day
Editor: Margaret Bam

For My Sons, Daniel, David and Jude

Wall of China, Jinshanling, China

China

China is a **country**.

A country is land that is controlled by a **single government**. Countries are also called **nations, states, or nation-states**.

Countries can be **different sizes**. Some countries are big and others are small.

Guiyang, China

Where Is China?

China is located in the continent of Asia.

A continent is a massive area of land that is separated from others by water or other natural features.

China is situated in East Asia.

Zhengyang Gate in Qianmen Street, Beijing

Capital

The capital of China is **Beijing.**

Beijing is located in the northern part of China.

Shanghai is the largest city in China by population.

Liede Bridge, Guangzhou, China

Provinces

China is divided into 23 provinces.

The provinces of China are:

Anhui, Fujian, Gansu, Guangdong, Guizhou, Hainan, Hebei, Heilongjiang, Henan, Hubei, Hunan, Jiangsu, Jiangxi, Jilin, Liaoning, Qinghai, Shaanxi, Shandong, Shanxi, Sichuan, Yunnan, and Zhejiang.

Population

China has population of around **1.4 billion people** making it the most populated country in the world.

Tiananmen Square, Beijing, China

Size

China is **9,596,961 square kilometres** making it the largest country in East Asia by area.

China is the second largest country in the world.

Languages

The official language of China is **Standard Chinese or Mandarin**. Mandarin is spoken by over 1.4 billion people in the world making it the second most spoken language in the world after English.

Here are a few Chinese phrases
- **Nǐhǎo** - Hello
- **Xièxiè** - Thank you
- **Bù kèqì** - You're welcome
- **Zǎo** - Good morning

Potala Palace

Attractions

There are lots of interesting places to see in China.

Some beautiful places to visit in China are

- Great Wall of China
- Emperor Qinshihuang's Mausoleum Site Museum
- Summer Palace
- The Bund
- The Palace Museum
- Potala Palace

China Shenzhen Skyscraper

History of China

People have lived in China for a very long time. In fact, China is regarded as one of the world's oldest civilisations. There is evidence that hominids inhabited the country from as far back as 2.25 million years ago.

On 1 January 1912, the Republic of China was established, and Sun Yat-sen of the Kuomintang was proclaimed provisional president.

Group of Chinese women

Customs in China

China has many fascinating customs and traditions.

- In China, burping after a meal is considered to be a display of gratitude and is considered a compliment to the chef.
- When giving a person a gift, it is expected that the intended recipient refuse the first few offers before accepting it.
- In some parts of China, domesticated geese are used by law enforcement.

Chinese Lion Dance

Music of China

There are many different music genres in China such as **Chinese classical music, C-pop, Chinese opera, Japanese rock, Mandopop and Guoyue.**

Some notable Chinese musicians include
- **Xian Xinghai**
- **Faye Wong**
- **Cui Jian**
- **Lang Lang**
- **Lu Han**
- **Wang Leehom**

Peking Duck

Food of China

China is known for its delicious, flavoursome and diverse food.

The national dish of China is **Peking Duck** which is a delicious duck dish known for its very crispy skin and beautiful caramel colour.

Kung Pao Chicken

Food of China

Some popular dishes in China include

- **Kung Pao Chicken**
- **Sweet and Sour Pork**
- **Mapo Tofu**
- **Chow Mein**
- **Chinese hot pot**

Chongsheng Monastery, China

Weather in China

The climate of China varies greatly across the country. While Southern China has a tropical climate, with high temperatures and heavy rainfall, the mountainous regions of Southwestern China experience more moderate temperatures.

Animals of China

There are many wonderful animals in China.

Here are some animals that live in China

- Giant pandas
- Tibetan macaques
- Chinese giant salamanders
- Golden snub-nosed monkeys
- Chinese sturgeons
- The red panda
- Siberian tiger

Lingyin Temple, China

Temples

There are many beautiful Temples in China which is one of the reasons why so many people visit this beautiful country every year.

Here are some of China's temples

- White Horse Temple
- Lingyin Temple
- Jokhang Temple
- Lama Temple
- Shaolin Temple

Nanjing Street, Shanghai

Sports of China

Sports play an integral part in Chinese culture. The most popular sport is **Basketball.**

Here are some of famous sportspeople from China

- **Liang Wen-Chong - Golf**
- **Yi Jianlian - Basketball**
- **Ma Long - Ping Pong**
- **Zou Kai - Gymnastics**

Confucius

Famous

Many successful people hail from China.

Here are some notable Chinese figures

- **Confucius – Philosopher**
- **Yao Ming – Basketball player**
- **Dilraba Dilmurat – Actress**
- **Deng Xiaoping – Politician**
- **Fan Bingbing – Actress**

Wuhua House, Yunnan, China

Something Extra...

As a little something extra, we are going to share some lesser known facts about Japan.

- In Chinese mythology, a monster called "Nian" comes out to eat people on New Year's Eve
- Facebook is banned in China.
- China is home to the world's biggest mall.

Words From the Author

We hope that you enjoyed learning about the wonderful country of China.

China is a country rich in culture and beauty, with lots of wonderful places to visit and people to meet.

We hope you continue to learn more about this wonderful nation. If you enjoyed this book, consider leaving a review!

With Love

Printed in Great Britain
by Amazon

55005548R00027